Golden Moments

Treasures of Inspiration

Golden Moments

by Henry van Dyke, Author of
'The Other Wise Man'

Edited by Marianne Wilson
and Peter Seymour
Illustrated by James R. Smith

♛ Hallmark Editions

Golden Moments

The Little
Friendship Fire

There are times and seasons when the angler has no need of the camp-fire, or the smudge-fire, or the cooking-fire. He sleeps in a house. His breakfast and dinner are cooked for him in a kitchen. He is in no great danger from black-flies or mosquitoes. All he needs now, as he sets out to spend a day on the Neversink, or the Willowemoc, or the Shepaug, or the Swiftwater, is a good lunch in his pocket, and a little friendship-fire to burn pleasantly beside him while he eats his frugal fare and prolongs his noon-day rest.

This form of fire does less work than any other in the world. Yet it is far from being useless; and I, for one, should be sorry to live without it. Its only use is to make a visible center of interest where there are two or three anglers eating their lunch together, or to supply a kind of companionship to a lone fisherman. It is kindled and burns for no other purpose than to give you the sense of being at home and at ease. Why the fire should do this, I cannot tell, but it does.

A man moves slowly or swiftly,
he does his work weakly or strongly,
according to the energy that is in him.
But the direction of his life,
                this way or that way,
follows the unseen influence
        of what he admires and loves
                and believes in.

Courage does not consist
                in the absence of fear,
but in the conquest of it.

The mother of poets is the Earth;
their father is the Great Spirit.

Talkability

"Talkable" is not a new adjective. But it needs a new definition, and the complement of a corresponding noun. I would fain set down on paper some observations and reflections which may serve to make its meaning clear, and render due praise to that most excellent quality in man or woman—the small but useful virtue of *talkability*. . . .

Now this good quality of talkability is to be distinguished, very strictly and inflexibly, from the bad quality which imitates it and often brings it into discredit. I mean the vice of talkativeness. That is a selfish, one-sided inharmonious affair, full of discomfort, and productive of most unchristian feelings. . . .

A talkative person is like an English sparrow—a bird that cannot sing, and will sing, and ought to be persuaded not to try to sing. But a talkable person has the gift that belongs to the wood thrush and the veery and the wren, the oriole and the white-throat and the rose-breasted grosbeak, and the mocking bird and the robin (sometimes); and the brown thrush; yes, the brown thrush has it to perfection, if you can catch him alone—the gift of being interesting, charming, delightful, in the most offhand and various modes of utterance. . . .

Talk is that form of human speech which is exempt from all duties, foreign and domestic. It is the nearest thing in the world to thinking and feeling aloud. It is necessarily not for publication—solely an evidence of good faith and mutual kindness. You tell me what you have seen and what you are thinking about, because you take it for granted that it will interest and entertain me; and you listen to my replies and the recital of my adventures and opinions, because you know I like to tell them, and because you find something in them, of one kind or another, that you care to hear. It is a nice game, with easy, simple rules, and endless possibilities of variation. And if we go into it with the right spirit, and play it for love, without heavy stakes, the chances are that if we happen to be fairly talkable people we shall have one of the best things in the world—a mighty good talk. . . .

The order in which you set out upon a talk, the path which you pursue, the rules which you observe or disregard, make but little difference in the end. You may follow the advice of Immanuel Kant if you like, and begin with the weather and the roads, and go on to current events, and wind up with history, art, and philosophy. Or you may reverse the order if you prefer, like that admirable talker Clarence King [American geologist and explorer], who usually set sail on some highly abstract paradox, such as "Civilization is a nervous disease," and landed in a tale of adventure in Mexico or the Rocky Mountains. Or you may follow the example of Edward Eggleston [minister and author], who started in at the middle and worked out at either end and sometimes at both. It makes no difference. If the thing is in you at all, you will find good matter for talk anywhere along the route. Hear what Montaigne says again: "In our discourse all subjects are alike to me; let there be neither weight nor depth, 'tis all one; there is yet grace and pertinence; all there is tinted with a mature and constant judgment, and mixed with goodness, freedom, gaiety, and friendship."

How close to the mark the old essayist sent his arrow! He is right about the essential qualities of good talk. They are not merely intellectual. They are moral. Goodness of heart, freedom of spirit, gaiety of temper, and friendliness of disposition—these are four fine things and doubtless as acceptable to God as they are agreeable to men. The talkability which springs out of these qualities has its roots in a good soil. On such a plant one need not look for the poison berries of malign discourse, nor for the Dead Sea apples of frivolous mockery. But fair fruit will be there, pleasant to the sight and good for food, brought forth abundantly according to the season. . . .

The very best thing in good talk, and the thing that helps it most, is *friendship*. How it dissolves the barriers that divide us, and loosens all constraint, and diffuses itself like some fine old cordial through all the veins of life—this feeling that we understand and trust each other, and wish each other heartily well! Everything into which it really comes is good. It transforms letter-writing from a task into a pleasure. It makes music a thousand times more sweet. The people who play and sing not *at* us, but *to* us—how delightful it is to listen to them! Yes, there is a talkability that can express itself even without words. There is an exchange of thought and feeling which is happy alike in speech and in silence. It is quietness pervaded with friendship.

Tribulation means "grinding";
and I suppose we must go through it
        if we want the good flour
                to come out of the wheat.

The one thing
        that we need to learn now
                is how to live
so that the first volume shall be good
        and the second
shall have the promise of being better.

Let a man live now
        in the light of the knowledge
                that he is to live forever.

Fisherman's Luck

I have often wished that every human employment might evolve its own appropriate greeting. Some of them would be queer, no doubt; but at least they would be an improvement on the wearisome iteration of "Good evening" and "Good morning," and the monotonous inquiry, "How do you do?"—a question so meaningless that it seldom tarries for an answer. Under the new and more natural system of etiquette, when you passed the time of day with a man you would know his business, and the salutations of the marketplace would be full of interest.

As for my chosen pursuit of angling (which I follow with diligence when not interrupted by less important concerns), I rejoice with every true fisherman that it has a greeting all its own and of a most honorable antiquity. There is no written record of its origin. But it is quite certain that since the days after the Flood, when Deucalion

Did first this art invent
Of angling, and his people taught the same,
two honest and good-natured anglers have never
met each other by the way without crying out,
"What luck?"

Here, indeed, is an epitome of the gentle art.

Here is the spirit of it embodied in a word and paying its respects to you with its native accent. Here you see its secret charms unconsciously disclosed. The attraction of angling for all the ages of man, from the cradle to the grave, lies in its uncertainty. 'Tis an affair of luck. . . .

Look at those two venerable gentlemen floating in a skiff upon the clear waters of Lake George. . . . They do not know at this moment whether the next turn of Fortune's reel will bring up a perch or a pickerel, a sunfish or a black bass. It may be a hideous catfish or a squirming eel, or it may be a lake-trout, the grand prize in the Lake George lottery. There they sit, those gray-haired lads, full of hope, yet equally prepared for resignation; taking no thought for the morrow, and ready to make the best of today; harmless and happy players at the best of all games of chance.

"In other words," I hear some severe and sour-complexioned reader say, "in plain language, they are a pair of old gamblers."

Yes, if it pleases you to call honest men by a bad name. But they risk nothing that is not their own; and if they lose, they are not impoverished. They desire nothing that belongs to other men; and if they win, no one is robbed. If all gambling were like that, it would be difficult to see the harm in it.

Indeed, a daring moralist might even assert, and prove by argument, that so innocent a delight in the taking of chances is an aid to virtue. . . .

I would not have you to suppose, gentle reader, that in discoursing of fisherman's luck I have in mind only those things which may be taken with a hook. It is a parable of human experience. I have been thinking, for instance, of Isaac Walton's life as well as of his angling: of the losses and sufferings that he, the firm Royalist, endured when the Commonwealth men came marching into London town; of the consoling days that were granted to him, in troublous times, on the banks of the Lea and the Dove and the New River, and the good friends that he made there, with whom he took sweet counsel in adversity; of the little children who played in his house for a few years, and then were called away into the silent land where he could hear their voices no longer. I was thinking how quietly and peaceably he lived through it all, not complaining nor desponding, but trying to do his work well, whether he was keeping a shop or writing books, and seeking to prove himself an honest man and a cheerful companion, and never scorning to take with a thankful heart such small comforts and recreations as came to him.

It is a plain, homely, old-fashioned meditation,

reader, but not unprofitable. *When I talk to you of fisherman's luck, I do not forget that there are deeper things behind it. I remember that what we call our fortunes, good or ill, are but the wise dealings and distributions of a Wisdom higher, and a Kindness greater, than our own.* And I suppose that their meaning is that we should learn, by all the uncertainties of our life, even the smallest, how to be brave and steady and temperate and hopeful, whatever comes, because we believe that behind it all there lies a purpose of good, and over it all there watches a providence of blessing.

If our education would but create

    a race of readers,

        earnest, intelligent,

   capable of true imaginative effort,

then the old writers

    would not be forgotten,

and the new ones would get

    a wiser welcome when they arrive.

We must ask if we would receive,
      we must seek if we would find.
We must knock
      if we desire to have the door
           of heaven opened to us.

The statesman
      who always follows public opinion
is a pilot
      who always steers with the tide.
He doesn't earn his fee.

The Lord God is our sun,
      and while He shines
we are happy and the world is bright.

Memories

Memory is a capricious and arbitrary creature. You never can tell what pebble she will pick up from the shore of life to keep among her treasures, or what inconspicuous flower of the field she will preserve as the symbol of

Thoughts that do often lie too deep for tears.

She has her own scale of values for these mementoes, and knows nothing of the market price of precious stones or the costly splendour of rare orchids. The thing that pleases her is the thing that she will hold fast. And yet I do not doubt that the most important things are always the best remembered; only we must learn that the real importance of what we see and hear in the world is to be measured at last by its meaning, its significance, its intimacy with the heart of our heart and the life of our life. And when we find a little token of the past very safely and imperishably kept among our recollections, we must believe that memory has made no mistake. It is because that little thing has entered into our experience most deeply, that it stays with us and we cannot lose it.

You have half forgotten many a famous scene that you travelled far to look upon. You cannot clearly recall the sublime peak of Mont Blanc, the roaring curve of Niagara, the vast dome of St. Peter's. The music of Patti's crystalline voice has left no distinct echo in your remembrance, and the blossoming of the century-plant is dimmer than the shadow of a dream. But there is a nameless valley among the hills where you can still trace every curve of the stream, and see the foam-bells floating on the pool below the bridge, and the long moss wavering in the current. There is a rustic song of a girl passing through the fields at sunset, that still repeats its far-off cadence in your listening ears. There is a small flower trembling on its stem in some hidden nook beneath the open sky, that never withers through all the changing years; the wind passes over it, but it is not gone—it abides forever in your soul, an amaranthine blossom of beauty and truth.

There is no duty so small,

    no trial so slight,

    that it does not

        afford room for courage.

Little Rivers

A river is the most human and companionable of all inanimate things. It has a life, a character, a voice of its own, and is as full of good fellowship as a sugar-maple is of sap. It can talk in various tones, loud or low, and of many subjects, grave and gay. Under favourable circumstances it will even make a shift to sing, not in a fashion that can be reduced to notes and set down in black and white on a sheet of paper, but in a vague, refreshing manner, and to a wandering air that goes

"Over the hills and far away."

For real company and friendship, there is nothing outside of the animal kingdom that is comparable to a river. . . .

The life of a river, like that of a human being, consists in the union of soul and body, the water and the banks. They belong together. They act and react upon each other. The stream moulds and makes the shore; hollowing out a bay here, and building a long point there; alluring the little bushes close to its side, and bending the tall slim trees over its current; sweeping a rocky ledge clean of everything but moss, and sending a still lagoon full of white arrow-heads and rosy knotweed far back into the meadow. The shore guides and controls the stream; now detaining and now advancing it; now bending it in a hundred sinuous curves, and now speeding it straight as a wild-bee on its homeward flight; here hiding the water in a deep cleft over-hung with green branches, and there spreading it out, like a mirror framed in daisies, to reflect the sky and clouds; sometimes breaking it with sudden turns and unexpected falls into a foam of musical laughter, sometimes soothing it into a sleepy motion like the flow of a dream. . . .

The real way to know a little river is not to glance at it here or there in the course of a hasty journey, nor to become acquainted with it after it has been partly civilized and spoiled by too close contact with the works of man. You must go to its native haunts; you must see it in youth and free-dom; you must accommodate yourself to its pace, and give yourself to its influence, and follow its meanderings whithersoever they may lead you.

Now, of this pleasant pastime there are three principal forms. You may go as a walker, taking the riverside path, or making a way for yourself through the tangled thickets or across the open meadows. You may go as a sailor, launching your light canoe on the swift current and committing yourself for a day, or a week, or a month, to the delightful uncertainties of a voyage through the forest. You may go as a wader, stepping into the stream and going down with it, through rapids and shallows and deeper pools, until you come to the end of your courage and the daylight. Of these three ways I know not which is best. But in all of them the essential thing is that you must be willing and glad to be led; you must take the little river for your guide, philosopher, and friend.

Nothing's lost that love remembers.

The heart of man,
  which can win such victory
    out of its darkest defeat
and reap such harvest
  from the furrows of the grave,
is neither sprung from dust
  nor destined to return to it.

A Wild Strawberry

Some day, I suppose, all things in the heavens above, and in the earth beneath, and in the hearts of the men and women who dwell between, will be investigated and explained. We shall live a perfectly ordered life, with no accidents, happy or unhappy. Everybody will act according to rule, and there will be no dotted lines on the map of human existence, no regions marked "unexplored." Perhaps that golden age of the machine will come, but you and I will hardly live to see it. And if that seems to you a matter for tears, you must do your own weeping, for I cannot find it in my heart to add a single drop of regret.

The results of education and social discipline in humanity are fine. It is a good thing that we can count upon them. But at the same time let us rejoice in the play of native traits and individual vagaries. Cultivated manners are admirable, yet there is a sudden touch of inborn grace and courtesy that goes beyond them all. No array of accomplishments can rival the charm of an unsuspected gift of nature, brought suddenly to light. I once heard a peasant girl singing down the Traunthal, and the echo of her song outlives, in the hearing of my heart, all memories of the grand opera.

The harvest of the gardens and the orchards, the result of prudent planting and patient cultivation, is full of satisfaction. We anticipate it in due season, and when it comes we fill our mouths and are grateful. But pray, kind Providence, let me slip over the fence out of the garden now and then, to shake a nut-tree that grows untended in the wood. Give me liberty to put off my black coat for a day, and go a-fishing on a free stream, and find by chance a wild strawberry.

A peace which depends upon fear

is nothing but a suppressed war.

Prayer is an instinct of the human heart, and the religion

which did not provide for it

would be no religion at all.

Every possible form of government
has been tried,
and found both good and bad.
They would all be intolerable
but for the quiet people
who trust in the Lord and do good.

Let us not pray chiefly
that God would let us into Heaven,
but first
that he would send Heaven into us.

Why quarrel about the social order?
It is the social spirit
that makes the difference.

'For Ye Are Bought With a Price' ST. PAUL

What is liberty? It is the recognition of voluntary allegiance to the highest law. And what is the highest law? It is the law of gratitude and love. Who, then, is free? He who sees and feels the obligations which bind him to serve the highest and the best.

The noblest, richest, fullest, purest life is that which has the deepest and strongest sense of indebtedness resting upon it always, and impelling it forward along the line of duty, which is also the line of joy. So, then, true liberty is the highest kind of bondage. . . .

I. *The sense of belonging to something is essential to our happiness.*

We are never without this sense, and therefore we do not realize its importance. But let us try for once to strip it away from us, and then perhaps we may feel what it means. You remember the story of "The Man Without a Country." Endeavor now to construct in imagination the figure of a man without a world, without a fellow-man, without a God. . . .

Does not the mere contemplation of such a condition as that throw us back forcibly, almost violently, upon the truth that the joy of life is a dependent joy, and that we can only come into true and happy possession of ourselves when we realize that we belong to something greater than ourselves? As living beings we are part of a universe of life; as intelligent beings we are in connection with a great circle of conscious intelligences; as spiritual beings we have our place in a moral world controlled and governed by the supreme Spirit. In each of these spheres there is a law, a duty, an obligation, a responsibility, for us. And our felicity lies in the discovery and acknowledgment of those ties which fit us and bind us to take our place, to play our part, to do our work, to live our life, where we belong.

II. This leads us on at once to the second proposition about life. *The true uplifting and emancipation of our life comes through the recognition of the higher ties and relationships which bind us. . . .*

Here is a slave bound by artificial law to the service of a human master. How shall you make that man free? Suppose you slay the master, and strike the bonds from the limbs of the slave, and say to him, "Go! you are free, you have no master, you belong to nobody." What have you done for him? Is he really any more free than he was before? Is he not still a slave, though a masterless one? But sup-

pose you teach him to believe that he is a human being, and that he has a service to render, even in his
low estate, to the whole brotherhood of mankind—
a service just as real and true, and therefore just as
noble, as that of the king upon the throne. Suppose
you bring into his mind the great truth that he belongs to God just as fully and as completely as his
master does, and that, even under the hard conditions of his life, it is his duty, his privilege, his
glory, to serve God by honesty and fidelity and diligence and purity. Now, indeed, you have liberated
his soul; and if the liberation of his body comes, as
it ought to come, as it must come, it will find him
already a free man, and fit for liberty, because he
has caught sight of the true meaning of fraternity
and equality. . . .

And so the Gospel carries written upon its very
face the great truth that the only real deliverance
from a lower bondage lies in the recognition of a
higher obligation.

Men are made free by discerning their noblest
allegiance.

III. But there is yet one more truth: *The inward
joy and power of our life, in every sphere, come
from the discovery that its highest obligation rests
at last upon the law of gratitude.* In every tie that
binds us, we are made free and glad to serve, when

we recognize that we have been "bought with a price." ...

Suppose we come to understand that this race of man to which we belong is bound together by something deeper and more vital than subjection to an outward law, that there is a vicarious element in human life, that no man liveth to himself and no man dieth to himself, that all the efforts and aspirations and toils and sufferings of humanity serve us and are for our sake. This is true in the plainest and most literal sense. The houses that shelter us, the clothes that cover us, the food on our tables, have all been won for us by the labour of other hands. We have paid for that labour, it is true, but there is one thing that we have not paid for, and that is the life that has gone into the labour. ...

Every touch of beauty, of light, of power, every gift of riches, of freedom, of learning that is ours, has been paid for by the lives of our fellow-men, and binds us to their service. It is this thought alone which can reveal to us the immense meaning of humanity, and fit us for our part in life, and make us truly noble men and gentle women. We are bought with a price.

Who Owns
the Mountains?

It was the little lad who asked the question; and the answer also, as you will see, was mainly his. . . .

Said the lad, lying on the grass beside me, "Father, who owns the mountains?"

I happened to have heard, the day before, of two or three lumber companies that had bought some of the woodland slopes; so I told him their names, adding that there were probably a good many different owners, whose claims taken all together would cover the whole Franconia range of hills.

"Well," answered the lad, after a moment of silence, "I don't see what difference that makes. Everybody can look at them."

They lay stretched out before us in the level sunlight, the sharp peaks outlined against the sky, the vast ridges of forest sinking smoothly toward the valleys, the deep hollows gathering purple shadows in their bosoms, and the little foothills standing out in rounded promontories of brighter green from the darker mass behind them. . . .

They were all ours, from crested cliff to wooded base. The solemn groves of firs and spruces, the plumed sierras of lofty pines, the stately pillared forests of birch and beech, the wild ravines, the tremulous thickets of silvery poplar, the bare peaks with their wide outlooks and the cool vales resounding with the ceaseless song of little rivers— we knew and loved them all; they ministered peace and joy to us; they were all ours, though we held no title deeds and our ownership had never been recorded.

What is property, after all? The law says there are two kinds, real and personal. But it seems to me that the only real property is that which is truly personal, that which we take into our inner life and make our own forever, by understanding and admiration and sympathy and love. This is the only kind of possession that is worth anything. . . .

We measure success by accumulation. The measure is false. The true measure is appreciation. He who loves most has most. . . .

"Come, laddie," I said to my comrade, "let us go home. *You and I are very rich. We own the mountains. But we can never sell them, and we don't want to.*"

Men are made free
by discerning their noblest allegiance.

Love is life,
and they who do not love are not alive.
But every soul that loves
lives in the heart of God
and hears Him speak.

The Bible does not profess
to make men omniscient,
but simply to tell them enough
to make them happy and good,
if they will believe it
and live up to it.

35

Dryads, Naiads,
and Oreads

The trim plantations of trees which are called "forests" in certain parts of Europe—scientifically pruned and tended, counted every year by uniformed foresters, and defended against all possible depredations—are admirable and useful in their way; but they lack the mystic enchantment of the fragments of native woodland which linger among the Adirondacks and the White Mountains, or the vast, shaggy, sylvan wildernesses which hide the lakes and rivers of Canada. These Laurentian Hills lie in No Man's Land. Here you do not need to keep to the path, for there is none. You may make your own trail, whithersoever fancy leads you; and at night you may pitch your tent under any tree that looks friendly and firm.

Here, if anywhere, you shall find Dryads, and Naiads, and Oreads. And if you chance to see one, by moonlight, combing her long hair beside the glimmering waterfall, or slipping silently, with gleaming shoulders, through the grove of silver birches, you may call her by the name that pleases you best. She is all your own discovery. There is no social directory in the wilderness.

One side of our nature, no doubt, finds its satisfaction in the regular, the proper, the conventional. But there is another side of our nature, underneath, that takes delight in the strange, the free, the spontaneous. We like to discover what we call a law of Nature, and make our calculations about it, and harness the force which lies behind it for our own purposes. But we taste a different kind of joy when an event occurs which nobody has foreseen or counted upon. It seems like an evidence that there is something in the world which is alive and mysterious and untrammelled.

Faith is an adventure;

it is the courage of the soul

to face the unknown.

But that courage springs

from the hope and confidence

of the soul

that its adventure will succeed.

All faith recognizes
        that life is a pilgrimage
whose course and duration
        cannot be foreseen.

There are two good rules
        which ought to be written
        upon every heart.
Never believe anything bad
        about anybody,
        unless you positively know
                that it is true.
Never tell even that, unless you feel
        that it is absolutely necessary,
        and that God is listening
                while you tell it.

The Haven of Character

Our life is made up, not of actions alone, but of thoughts and feelings and habitual affections. These taken all together constitute what we call our present character. In their tendencies and impulses and dominant desires they constitute our future character, towards which we are moving as a ship to her haven.

What is it, then, for you and me, this intimate ideal, this distant self, this hidden form of personality which is our goal?

I am sure that we do not often enough put the problem clearly before us in this shape. We all dream of the future, especially when we are young.

A boy's will is the wind's will,
And the thoughts of youth are long, long
thoughts. . . .

The stuff of which our day-dreams are made is for the most part of very cheap material. We seldom weave into them the threads of our inmost spiritual life. We build castles in Spain, and forecast adventures in Bohemia. But the castle is without a real master. The hero of the adventure is vague and misty. We do not clearly recognize his face, or know what is in his heart. . . .

But in all these reveries we do not really think deeply of our Selves. We do not stay to ask what manner of men and women we shall be, when we are living here or there, or doing thus or so.

Yet it is an important question—very much more important, in fact, than the thousand and one trifling interrogatories about the future with which we amuse our idle hours.

And the strange thing is that, though our ideal of future character is so often hidden from us, over-looked, forgotten, it is always there, and always potently, though unconsciously, shaping our course in life. "Every one," says Cervantes, "is the son of his own works." But his works do not come out of the air, by chance. They are wrought out in a secret, instinctive harmony with a conception of character which we inwardly acknowledge as possible and likely for us.

When we choose between two lines of conduct, between a mean action and a noble one, we choose also between two persons, both bearing our name, the one representing what is best in us, the other embodying what is worst. When we vacillate and alternate between them, we veer, as the man in Robert Louis Stevenson's story veered, between Dr.

Jekyll and Mr. Hyde.

We say that we "make up our minds" to do a certain thing or not to do it, to resist a certain temptation or to yield to it. It is true. We "make up our minds" in a deeper sense than we remember. In every case the ultimate decision is between two future selves, one with whom the virtue is harmonious, another with whom the vice is consistent. To one of these two figures, dimly concealed behind the action, we move forward. What we forget is that, when the forward step is taken, the shadow will be *myself*. Character is eternal destiny.

The man who thinks when old

precisely the same on all points

      as he thought when young

           is not a conservative.

He is an obstacle.

Often the simple things
     are the hardest,
     because they leave no room
        for deception.

Democracy can never be extended
     by force, as you would fling a net
        over a flock of birds;
but give it a chance and it will grow,
     by sending down its roots
        into the heart of humanity
and lifting its top toward the light
and spreading its arms wider
     and wider
until all the persecuted flocks of heaven
find refuge beneath its protecting shade.

'The Question of Life'

What is the goal that you desire and hope to reach? What is the end of life towards which you are drifting or steering?

There are three ways in which we may look at this question, depending upon the point of view from which we regard human existence.

When we think of it as a work, the question is, "What do we desire to accomplish?"

When we think of it as a growth, a development, a personal unfolding, the question is, "What do we desire to become?"

When we think of it as an experience, a destiny, the question is, "What do we desire to become of us?" . . .

There is a difference in these three standpoints from which we may look at our life; and this difference not only makes a little variation in the view that we take of our existence, but also influences unconsciously our manner of thinking and speaking about it. Most of the misunderstandings that arise when we are talking about life come from a failure to remember this. We are looking at the same thing, but we are looking from opposite corners of the room. We are discussing the same subject, but in different dialects.

Some people—perhaps the majority—are of a practical turn of mind. Life seems to them principally an affair of definite labour directed to certain positive results. They are usually thinking about what they are to do in the world, and what they are to get for it. It is a question of occupation, of accomplishment, of work and wages.

Other people—and I think almost all serious-minded people when they are young, and life still appears fresh and wonderful to them—regard their existence from the standpoint of sentiment, of feeling, of personality. They have their favourite characters in history or fiction, whom they admire and try to imitate. They have their ideals, which they seek and hope to realize. Some vision of triumph over obstacles, and victory over enemies, some model of manhood or womanhood, shines before them. By that standard they test and measure themselves. Towards that end they direct their efforts. The question of life, for them, is a question of attainment, of self-discipline, of self-development.

Other people—and I suppose we may say all people at some time or other in their experience—catch a glimpse of life in still wider and more mysterious relations. They see that it is not really, for any one of us, an independent and self-centered and self-controlled affair. They feel that its issues run out far beyond what we can see in this world. They have a deep sense of a future state of being towards which we are all inevitably moving. This movement cannot be a matter of chance. It must be under law, under responsibility, under guidance. It cannot be a matter of indifference to us. It ought to be the object of our most earnest concern, our most careful choice, our most determined endeavour. *If there is a port beyond the horizon, we should know where it lies and how to win it. And so the question of life, in these profound moods which come to all of us, presents itself as a question of eternal destiny.*

It is said that a man may be known

by the company he keeps.

Not always.

He may be better known

by the purpose with which he keeps it.

Men's little ways
        are usually more interesting,
and often more instructive
                than their grand manners.
When they are off guard,
        they frequently show
                to better advantage
than when they are on parade.

True liberty
        is the highest kind of bondage.

We do not know anything about God
        unless we know
that we cannot know Him perfectly.

Au Large!

There is magic in words, surely, and many a treasure besides Ali Baba's is unlocked with a verbal key. Some charm in the mere sound, some association with the pleasant past, touches a secret spring. The bars are down; the gate is open; you are made free of all the fields of memory and fancy—by a word.

Au large! Envoyez au large! is the cry of the Canadian voyagers as they thrust their paddles against the shore and push out on the broad lake for a journey through the wilderness. *Au large!* is what the man in the bow shouts to the man in the stern when the birch canoe is running down the rapids, and the water grows too broke, and the rocks too thick, along the river-bank. Then the frail bark must be driven out into the very center of the wild current, into the midst of danger to find safety, dashing, like a frightened colt, along the smooth, sloping lane bordered by white fences of foam.

Au large! When I hear that word, I hear also the crisp waves breaking on pebbly beaches, and the big wind rushing through innumerable trees, and the roar of headlong rivers leaping down the rocks. I see long reaches of water sparkling in the sun, or sleeping still between evergreen walls beneath a cloudy sky; and the gleam of white tents on the shore; and the glow of firelight dancing through the woods. I smell the delicate vanishing perfume of forest flowers; and the incense of rolls of birch-bark, crinkling and flaring in the campfire; and the soothing odor of balsam-boughs piled deep for woodland beds—the veritable and only genuine perfume of the land of Nod. The thin shining veil of the Northern lights waves and fades and brightens over the night sky; at the sound of the word, as at the ringing of a bell, the curtain rises. *Scene, the Forest of Arden; enter a party of hunters. . . .*

The strength of your life

      is measured by the strength

          of your will.

But the strength of your will

      is just the strength

      of the wish that lies behind it.

"Tact," said a witty lady,
    "is the unsaid part of what you think."
Yes, and there is only
one thing more potent — its opposite —
the unthought part of what you say.

The lesson which the life
                of Jesus teaches us
is that the only way
        to make the world better
        is for each man to do his best.

Where science ends,
        where philosophy pauses,
                faith begins.

There is a loftier ambition
than merely to stand high in the world.
It is to stoop down
    and lift mankind a little higher.

You will teach your children
    good principles more readily
than you will rid them of bad habits.

They who know the sorrows
    other lives have known,
        never walk alone.

Character is the compass of life.

Simplicity in Our Lives

There is a great complaint nowadays about the complication of life, especially in its social and material aspects. It is bewildering, confusing, overstraining. It destroys the temper of tranquility necessary to education. The simple life is recommended, and rightly, as a refuge from this trouble.

But perhaps we need to understand a little more clearly what simplicity is. It does not consist merely in the absence of *bric-a-brac....*

Simplicity, in truth, depends but little on external things. It is not outward, but inward. A certain openness of mind to learn the daily lessons of the school of life; a certain willingness of heart to give and to receive that extra service, that gift beyond the strict measure of debt, which makes friendship possible; a certain clearness of spirit to perceive the best in things and people, to love it without fear and to cleave to it without mistrust; a peaceable sureness of affection and taste; a gentle straightforwardness of action; a kind sincerity of speech— these are the marks of the simple life. It cometh not with observation, for it is within you. I have seen it in a hut. I have seen it in a palace. And wherever it is found it is the best prize of the school of life.

The real test of character is joy.
  For what you rejoice in,
      that you love.
  And what you love,
      that you grow to like.

[Good men] ought to be
like the tree of paradise,
      "whose leaves are for the healing
        of the nations."

Goodness is the purpose of religion,
      and its best proof.
Conduct is the end of faith,
      and its strongest support.

The Gift of Imagination

To see things as they are—that is a precious gift. To see things as they were in their beginning, or as they will be in their ending, or as they ought to be in their perfecting; to make the absent, present; to rebuild the past out of a fragment of carven stone; to foresee the future harvest in the grain of wheat in the sower's hand; to visualize the face of the invisible, and enter into the lives of all sorts and conditions of unknown men—that is a far more precious gift.

Imagination is more than a pleasant fountain; it is a fertilizing stream. *Nothing great has ever been discovered or invented without the aid of imagination. It is the medium of all human sympathy.* No man can feel with another unless he can imagine himself in the other man's place.

It is a pity

that men should be divided

by their pleasures

more than by their work.

Day's End

The lights in the cottages twinkle like fireflies, and there are small groups of people singing and laughing down the road. The honest fisherman reflects that this world is only a place of pilgrimage, but after all there is a good deal of cheer on the journey, if it is made with a contented heart. He wonders who the dwellers in the scattered houses may be, and weaves romances out of the shadows on the curtained windows. The lamps burning in the wayside shrines tell him stories of human love and patience and hope, and of divine forgiveness. Dream-pictures of life float before him, tender and luminous, filled with a vague, soft atmosphere in which the simplest outlines gain a strange significance. They are like some of Millet's paintings—"The Sower," or "The Sheepfold"—there is very little detail in them; but sometimes a little means so much.

Then the moon slips up into the sky from behind the eastern hills, and the fisherman begins to think of home, and of the foolish, fond old rhymes about those whom the moon sees far away, and the stars that have the power to fulfill wishes—as if the celestial bodies knew or cared anything about our small nerve-thrills which we call affection and de-sires! But if there were Some One above the moon and stars who did know and care, Some One who could see the places and the people that you and I would give so much to see, Some One who could do for them all of kindness that you and I fain would do, Some One able to keep our beloved in perfect peace and watch over the little children sleeping in their beds beyond the sea—what then? Why, then, in the evening hour, one might have thoughts of home that would go across the ocean by way of heaven, and be better than dreams, almost as good as prayers.

It is while we look

    that we learn to love.

It is by loving

    that we learn to seek.

And it is in seeking

    that we find and are blessed.

There is only one way
        to get ready for immortality,
and that is to love this life,
and live it as bravely
        and cheerfully and faithfully
                as we can.

If, as I believe,
life is the test of thought,
        rather than thought the test of life,
we should be able to get light
    on the real worth of a man's theories,
ideals, beliefs, by looking at the shape
        which they would give
                        to human existence
        if they were faithfully applied.

Traveling With Time

The wild desire to be forever racing against old Father Time is one of the kill-joys of modern life. That ancient traveler is sure to beat you in the long run, and as long as you are trying to rival him, he will make your life a burden. But if you will only acknowledge his superiority and profess that you do not approve of racing after all, he will settle down quietly beside you and jog along like the most companionable of creatures. That is a pleasant pilgrimage in which *the journey itself is part of the destination.*

Our life is not a mere fact;

it is a movement,

a tendency,

a steady, ceaseless progress

toward an unseen goal.

To desire and strive

        to be of some service

        to the world,

to aim at doing something

     which shall really

     increase the happiness and welfare

        and virtue of mankind —

this is a choice which is possible

        for all of us; and surely

it is a good haven to sail for.

Set in Linotype Aldus, a roman with old-face
characteristics, designed by Hermann Zapf.
Aldus was named for the 16th century Venetian
printer Aldus Manutius.
Typography by Grant Dahlstrom, set at
The Castle Press.
Printed on Hallmark Eggshell Book paper.
Designed by Jay D. Johnson.